Unicorn German Series ☙ Günter Bruno Fuchs

GÜNTER BRUNO FUCHS

LAW AND DISORDER

Poems & Pictures

Remarks by
Sparrows, Chimney Sweeps, Generals,
Old Kings, Madmen, Poets,
Dancers, Law Enforcers
&
Others

Translated by Richard Exner

UNICORN PRESS

UNICORN PRESS, INC.
P.O. BOX 3307
GREENSBORO, N.C. 27402

Editor's Foreword

GÜNTER BRUNO FUCHS, born in Berlin in 1928, has been variously described: in his own words as "drinker, poet, woodcutter," by his German publisher as "writer, poet, graphic artist, printer," by his biographers as having been, variously, circus clown, day laborer, prisoner of war, co-founder of an important Berlin art gallery. He has been called the German Prévert, but such a comparison is only apt, other than in a very general way, if one bears in mind that Prévert is essentially a *Parisian* poet and Fuchs a *Berlin* poet. For Fuchs is a unique phenomenon: his graphic work as well as his writings are filled with the laughter and gravity, grotesquerie and polish, irony and provocativeness, typical of Berliners. In his expressed endeavor to "stay close to the truth," he turns words and visual elements around and makes us see and listen in a new way. Because a mirror only reflects what we are accustomed to seeing, what we expect to see, Fuchs, through the words and images of his sparrows and owls, of his beast-man and man-bird, of his sword swallowers and chimney sweeps, tragic clowns and ridiculous bureaucrats, takes us through the looking-glass, where the grotesque becomes delightful, the serious becomes rebellious, the irony compassionate. This is the new surrealism: simple yet profound, committed but understated, quite German, very contemporary.

Since 1957, when his first full-length book of poems and graphics was published *(After the House Search)* and won him his first of many awards (the Baden Baden Youth Prize), he has been prolific, publishing almost annually, almost always collections of words and graphics. Recently, his poems have become prose-poems of a distinctive sort and his woodblocks, fables. Examples of his titles hint at his unique vision and style: *Humbug, A Sword Swallower's Prayer Book, The Kreuzberg Bar Dream of Mr. Owl, Crumb Pickers or 34 Chapters from the Life of Animal Imitator Ewald K., Itinerary for West Berliners....*

The poems for this selection of translations were chosen, by Richard Exner, from *Songs for Sleepers* (Pennergesang, 1965), *Leaves of a Court Poet and Other Verses* (Blätter eines Hof-Poeten & andere Gedichte, 1967), and the *Günter Bruno Fuchs Reader* (Lesebuch, 1970, all published by Carl Hanser Verlag, Munich.

The translater, in the opinion of this editor, has managed to adapt authentically into English the tone of the poems, even the Berlin "dialect" and the plays on words which Fuchs uses at times, while being faithful to the author's intent.

Günter Bruno Fuchs, poet and artist, died, tragically too soon, on April 19, 1977, while this book, his first to be published in English, was being translated.

Teo Savory

Contents

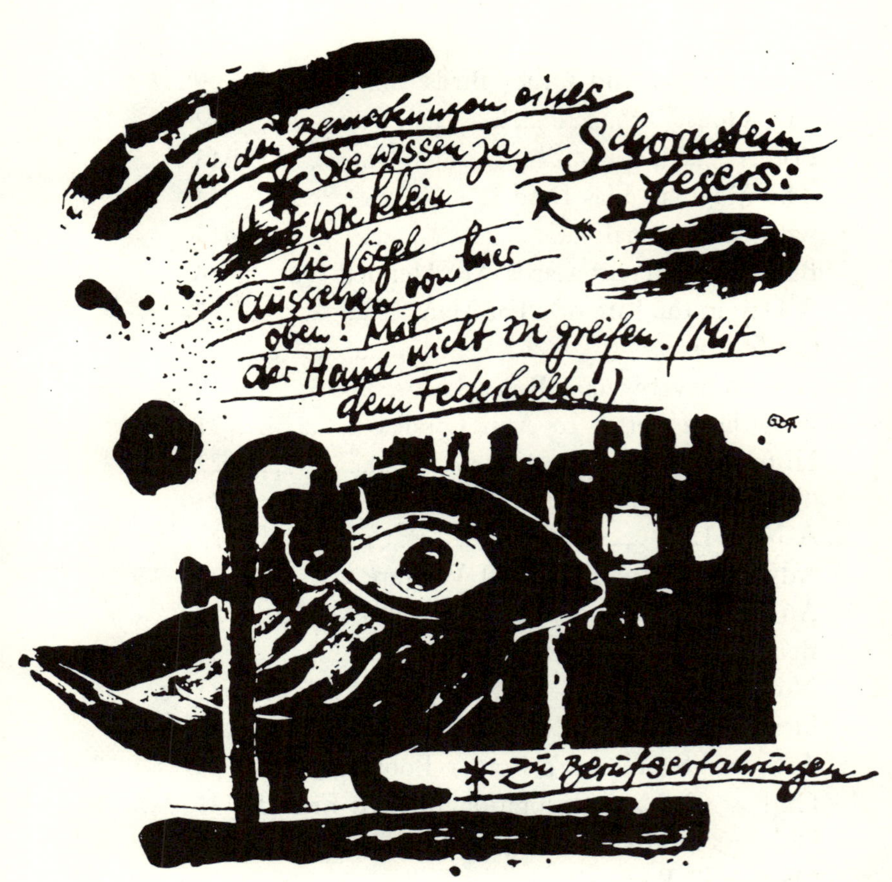
Aus den Bemerkungen eines
* Sie wissen ja, Schornstein-
so klein fegers:
die Vögel
aussehen von hier
oben! Mit der Hand nicht zu greifen. (Mit
dem Federhalter.)
* Zu Berufserfahrungen

The Sparrow and Other Birds

1

The sparrow
assumes janitorial duties
in the home of the big steamboat bell;
the same sparrow
rings his feathered keys:
Evening's here! Don't act surprised!
Other birds
look for jobs in downspouts,
pouring water onto firebrands;
still others
hop along the footpaths in the English Garden
and sleep very soundly
in the well-manicured spheres of trees.

2

The sparrow
loves to hatch in a street cleaner's cap.
This elicits praise from the municipal government
which then allots a pension to the sparrow.
Other birds
would much rather hatch in a child's bouncing ball.
A child is amazed
at how high his ball can fly.
The sparrow
is a polite bird. He yields
to horse-drawn carriages. His
eyes are translated into many languages.

3

Other birds
are no less polite,
they come to the theatre early
in time for the scene-shift
to a little forest.
Still other birds
serve as ferries between
bright river banks,
pavilions for plays and games,
festivals of flowers and dray horses.

The sparrow is a talented printer.
We owe this poem
to his art.
The same sparrow
heralds spring,
my rabbi
in the green synagogue.

The House

The house is gone.
Where is it? Did it just
take a little walk or did it
go looking for us?

Perhaps it will be back by
tomorrow. But how can it find its way
if no one opens
the eyes
of its windows?

Primer

1

What kind of man? A simple He.

2

What work? He read his primer steadily.

3

What did he read? I never heard.

4

Try to recall! It's too absurd:

5

For he and primer were interred.

The Madman Has Died

When the trains were late
he told stories
from the Thousand and One Nights
in the waiting room.

He never really learned
to say hello. If you said:
How are you? he always answered:
Perhaps.

We know he tipped his hat
to the dogs,
and the children took home
his royal crown made of newspaper.

A five-line local news item
concluded with the words:
On his last night
he climbed the tree in the park.

Rumor has it that he forgot
to hold on
when he delivered his peace message
to the world.

Fall Commercial

Ladies and gentlemen: here is the fall!
Every family's friend; housewives
love his thrifty consumption
of leaves. Fall never comes C.O.D.
and when you have had enough
you get your money back,
no questions asked. (Take a chance
on fall and use our easy monthly rates!)

*

Fashioned by the hand of a master,
fall need by no means pose
for antique walnut furniture.
After all, each of its creations
is more beautiful than the last.
Seven thousand bids, some in color.
Fall sees to law and order promptly,
and dreaming street cleaners receive answers
to many questions, free of charge.

Before the Report Cards Are Handed Out

The teacher says: the leaves fall
to the ground. What falls? Who or what
covers what or whom? You don't like that, do you,
if I ask whom or what do the leaves cover?
Well, the earth is covered by the leaves. The earth
and, besides, who or what? And when?
And how often? OK; now write
your essay on Fall.

A Day in the Life of a Fat Man

In the morning
he sells his services to the kids in the sandbox.
He begins work and says: Dear children,
this belly is not a belly but the great mountain of Bimboula.
The children laugh, turn somersaults, and say:
Please, great mountain, you must come back tomorrow.

At noon
he imitates his friends in the primeval forest.
He drums on his belly
and sometimes jumps, with a heavy heart,
onto a general's back and says:
If you should mistake my belly for a drum
that would be your tough luck. This belly
is really the great mountain of Bimboula
whose beauty you will never fathom.

At night
he is always very sad.
He sits down under the stars and
drinks twenty pints of sky beer;
some people hear him sing —
usually a very simple song,
so simple no one believes it:
O mother, mother, I'm hungry!

Confession

Ever since you left
I order two shots, not one.
After all, you might drop in at the bar —
why tip off the bartender: hey, my friend
has come back — bring another one!

And that's why I'm always drunk
ahead of time. And so that's why
I'll have to think up a new excuse
when you do
return.

A Chimney Sweep's Remarks

On Job Selection

As a child
I touched the stove
with both hands.
Thank you,
said the stove,
this gives my chimney
a warm feeling.

On One's General Condition

Have you
trouble with your
heart?
Yes, from old
air-raid sirens
on rooftops.

On the Times

They say confetti
could be black as soot.
Should we scatter black
confetti down onto the
Prime Minister
as he passes by?

On Professional Experience

You know, don't you,
how small the birds look
from up here!
Impossible to reach
by hand, feather,
or quill.

On Wage Questions

I love those houses
of mine; as chimney sweep
I know their insides
more intimately
than anyone.

On Old Age Pensions

Armed airplanes
are flown by
such people
as can be found
everywhere:
victims of
careless
job counseling.

A Father's Letter to Ann Landers

Dear Ann: actually our son was
supposed to take up refrigeration engineering
but somehow those strolls
with paper flowers interfered. (At twenty he
took part in a children's festival.)

Night after night I try to shake him
out of this nonsense. I make fun of him,
offer to slap his face, tell him to come to the window
and say, "Don't just stand there, do you like
our freeways or don't you?"

Last week he jumped onto the window sill, circled
Wilmersdorf seventeen times
and disappeared into the night.

In the morning (at breakfast) the same incomprehensible
stuff: how he had interviewed Mr. von Lilienthal
to whom the birds were indebted for flying
and people (during the last fifty years)
for airmailed greetings.

(What in hell is he saying? And how come he can fly?
Please answer. I am accustomed to facing
facts.)

Historic Places

1

Next time
you come into our town
bear left: nowhere else
such a gorgeous
office building!

2

Hello there, windmills!
My father Sancho Panza
has told me lots
about you.

3

We employ the unskilled!
Employ them, deploy them,
destroy them.
That's what they used to put
on recruiting posters
in hard times.

The Miller's Ballad

1

My father owned an ass, me (to be exact), who
was very lazy, too lazy to carry sacks and
similar burdens. Therefore my father said to me:
Anybody doesn't love our mill, I won't love him.
So, scram!

2

So I spent ten full years and thirty-five
seven-day weeks on this earth under a dark sun.
I confess not once did I want to sing
the song of the wandering miller, instead
I rather frequently sang the song of the
wandering ass.

3

The line *"The stones, despite their awful weight,
they wander too!"* got to me especially at first;
but by and by I enjoyed furnishing
the stones with hiking boots and scout manuals.
This was the start of my essay "Concerning Fun
From Ancient Times to the Present"; the present,
of course, hardly cares for such stories.

4

My presentation in the graduate seminar
(German Studies) would have been received
more kindly had I not continuously been
telling tales out of mill.

5

Today, this very hour,
I've come back. The mill is deserted,
my father nowhere to be seen. I ask all
of you: Where are all of you? The mill
is idle: I am waiting for you. Or
don't you eat real bread
anymore?

A New Law

*is said to enable generals legally to retain and look after
their dead for the rest of their lives*

1

The general retires, the new law troubles
him. He is living with
the dead; he buries each one, shapes every
mound with spade and shovel, plants
every flower and engraves every headstone —
stooping daily
morning, noon and night
he works among the graves, stooped
he works, nobody carries water, no one weeds
the paths, he walks them by himself,
narrowly, the weeds guiding him along,
he says: these weeds shoot at me, the dead
have sown them. The new law
troubles him.

2

The general lives with the dead. He is entitled to that.
He knows them all; they wake him early in the morning
when he is sleeping, face to the ground,
flat between the graves, dreaming of commands,
earth under his tongue; they all hear him,
they are faithful unto death, and that troubles him.

3

The general must look after his dead; he has led them,
he has kept his word, they all profited. No one
begrudges him this new law: the dead are his —
see him carry the water, he puts it on the mounds,
stooped, he works between the graves; he is entitled to that.

4

The general has become a benefactor.
Sincere, a man in his best years,
he calls for more graves which will need weeding.
He is exemplary, he helps wives and mothers,
he recognizes their power to deprive him of men
morning, noon, and night; daily in fact,
but they have forgotten his power,
their sons lie face to the ground,
earth under their tongues, no loss of sleep anymore:
there is dust on the windows, real trouble,
no carpet no home; it's obvious to every housewife.

5

The general retires, the new law
takes him back to the trenches,
he hears Verdun while summering as a tourist in Warsaw,
in the Russian steppes; he can feel how death
"falls in" to kill him for the rest of his life.
Therefore the general rejects the new law and
does not engrave headstones.

6

The general, the accommodating man of the hour,
faithful to his task of replenishing the earth with sons,
morning, noon and night; nightly in fact,
now, in this century, releases his smile:
*For the destruction of smaller cities medium-sized bombs
have done excellent service.* That's what he says,
cleverly, a first-class business-man.
And this label will fit for a little while longer.

Advice from the Bureau of Welfare

If you cannot find work,
please sleep or
hibernate. This will
provide you with the
rare opportunity
to get to know
some animals

An Old King Pores Over the Family Album

This is a picture of my owl and me. Taken many years ago.
I have no trouble recognizing us and remembering
how we felt in those days.

The picture shows a king
with a crown on his head and with cheerful eyes,
I see myself smile. The mouth
belongs to a man
who enjoys being king. My mantle is red,
doublet and hose are both blue,
my hands are folded, they had little to do
fingering the sceptre and an occasional gesture,
nothing to take up the attention of a ruler.
When this picture was snapped my subjects were
milling under the balcony—but let's leave that for the moment.

Immediately on my right: my owl, also merry-eyed.
He's no longer alive, and my crown is in mothballs.
How my owl would have enjoyed this!

All in all: quite a funny picture. (We really shouldn't
fuss about having been deposed.)

Being a Bird Takes Some Skill

1

The bird slept well in his birdhouse, opens his eyes and looks
forward to something very special: he says
water and birdseed are very special; he breakfasts on
water and birdseed. Such a breakfast is
cause for a happy dance; the bird reaches for his hat, lifts his
wings and takes off.

2

Flying he says: I am flying over some lovely country;
down there a human is having breakfast, I shall tell him:
You are fortunate to be able to eat breakfast
without having to wear a helmet
just as fortunate as a country where humans may speak,
look, and breakfast as freely as a bird.

3

Well, says the bird, no big deal but it
needed saying; such clarifications come under
the heading of freedom, in other words, just
like being a bird takes some skill.

Now in the Spring

Heinrich B., high-wire artist, traveling acrobat and
showman, with his wife, his brother, and two
school-aged children, moved last September
into the suburb of S. Fifty posters, none
larger than a newspaper, announced: Heinrich B.,
the man of the skies.

The first performance was scheduled for a Sunday,
Place: inside a vacant lot. The high-wire work,
climaxed by a handstand on several piled-up chairs,
was critically viewed by four people:
the wife, the brother, and the two school-aged children
of the high-wire artist Heinrich B. No other
spectators were in attendance.

Now in the spring
I discover one of the posters at the entrance of the coal dump;
no larger than a newspaper, it made it though the winter
announcing the man of the skies.

Identification

I live behind the steps of the policeman
who checks my passport.
I live in the basement of a medium-sized
ruin, in a rest home
for retired winds.

I live in the dangling cage
of a parrot who commits the law codes
to memory.

My residence
at the place of public disorder
is a circus on fire —
my wishes, traveling to you
on their hands,
are the last acrobats
under the blazing Big Top.

Sir, a lamp-post said to me, please believe me, I wanted to be a superior lamp-post. People have forgotten that I served as a gallows. The blood has never been washed off, and the dry rope is poisoning the wind. Please imagine: every night the same memory, the soldier under the gas light, feet stiff, tag on his chest.

I was not able to prevent the lamp-post from committing suicide. It uprooted its one leg from the pavement, and with absurdly short hops it reached the bridge. The clang against the railing! The cry of the fish! It fell head first into the canal.

*

Let's have some law and order, cried the anarchist, and tossed the bomb into City Hall.

*

When it starts to snow, the dogs, without training, dance on their hindlegs. They say: snow, snow, don't you go — from the big dog house in the sky, without any muzzle, stars fall and taste like bread.

Their laughing jaws clear a path through the snow mountain Earth; their jumps are silent barks, their lives fall with the snow from the heavens.

*

While earth was tossing in her sleep,
I saw the wars, all crouched, jump
from country to country, bombs and fuses
in their cloaks, like brigands in clown-white
make-up, in an operetta.

It did not dawn on me how dreadful this
deception was and how false this image
until I saw the earth, struck dead while
asleep, toss for the last time.

Cagliostro's Last Incantation for His Friends

Are we ready — have you gathered everything together — are the suit-cases packed, was nothing forgotten — not even the precious dragon hat which brings us the beautiful and refreshing rain?

I can see you have prepared everything; I shall go now. Remember the spell that reduces the coffins of old and new boredom to kindling. Bed down friend and enemy; they will not return when dust, the gravedigger, begins his journey.

Farewell! Baptised in the name of the clouds, I fly without travel permit over the assembled shades. I shall wear the dragon hat which brings us the beautiful and refreshing rain for I must pass through the fire which awaits me.

Dancer's Death

He comes down the street, they all recognize him, he waves a newspaper, he has read it, he leaps over cars, climbs along downspouts and cries: Folks, be happy with me, the Federal Hangman is back in office! Finally, our lives will have some purpose again. Now everyone knows why he must toil. His reward is assured. Come, come, repeat after me: Our heads belong to the hangman; he is the man of law and order!

They crowd together and chant: Who else . . . but to the man of law and order!

The dancer folds up his paper in amazement. They smile, they kiss and caress each other — a minuet of contentment. The dancer refuses to join them.

Instead he runs after them and cries: Listen to me, you took this too literally! Freedom will wither away and the truth will perish.

Now they turn on him and their hands become fists. They exclaim while beating him, you are insulting the Hangman, the man of compassion who has delivered us from freedom!

They smile again, kiss and caress, and the dancer dies amidst their thanksgiving.

"Wanted" Posters

1

Wanted: cleansing rains
to rinse the poison from our eyes.

Wanted: a child on stilts
to promise these rains a generous reward.

2

The window cleaner
leans his ladder against the dust-covered sky.
Autumn opens the synagogue,
storms chant the Torah.

Smoke signals by day.

The trees are old rabbis
lighting menorahs.

Fire signals by night.

Chains encircle the tree
where the crows sleep.
Your dreams are presaged by baying dogs.
A child's pinwheel
pronounces judgment on the world.

FABLES

Günter Bruno Fuchs

PATHS

SUN

Günter Brüno Fuchs / 1969

1 BEAR

REFUGE?

HIGHWAYMAN

FISH

Inhalt

Aus den Bemerkungen eines
* Sie wissen ja,   Schornstein-
wie klein   fegers:
die Vögel
aussehen von hier
oben! Mit
der Hand nicht zu greifen. (Mit
dem Federhalter.)
* Zu Berufserfahrungen

Der Sperling und andere Vögel

1

Der Sperling
übernimmt das Amt des Hausmeisters
im Haus der großen Dampferglocke.
Derselbe Sperling
läutet mit seinen gefiederten Schlüsseln:
Der Abend ist da, was wundert ihr euch!
Andere Vögel
suchen ihren Arbeitsplatz auf Regenrinnen,
sie schütten Wasser in die Feuersbrunst.
Wieder andere Vögel
hüpfen den Weg des Englischen Gartens entlang
und schlafen tief im gutfrisierten Kugelbaum.

2

Der Sperling
brütet gern in der Mütze eines Straßenfegers.
So erwirbt er das Lob der Stadtverwaltung —
sie setzt ihm ein Ruhegeld aus.
Andere Vögel
brüten am liebsten im Kinderball.
Ein Kind freut sich,
wie schön sein Ball hochfliegen kann.
Der Sperling
ist ein höflicher Vogel, er läßt den Pferdewagen
Freie Fahrt. Seine Augen
sind in viele Sprachen übersetzt.

3

Andere Vögel
erscheinen nicht minder höflich. Sie kommen früh
ins Theater, wenn ein Wäldchen auftreten muß.
Wieder andere Vögel
bereiten eine Fähre zwischen hellen Ufern,
den Pavillon der Spiele, ein Fest
der Blumen und Marktpferde.
Der Sperling
ist ein begabter Drucker. Seiner Kunst
verdanken wir dieses Gedicht.
Derselbe Sperling
sagt uns den Frühling an, mein Rabbi
in der grünen Synagoge.

Das Haus

Das Haus ist fort.
Wo ist das Haus geblieben? Wollte es nur
einen Spaziergang machen
oder ist es auf die Suche gegangen nach uns?

Vielleicht kehrt es schon morgen zurück.
Wie soll es zurückkehren,
da ihm niemand die Augen
die Fenster öffnet.

Fibel

1

Was war er denn? Er ist gewesen.

2

Was tat er denn? In einer Fibel lesen.

3

Was las er da? Ich weiß mehr.

4

Besinn dich doch! Ist schon zu lange her.

5

Die Fibel wurde eingescharrt wie er.

Der Irre ist gestorben

Im Wartesaal, wenn die Züge
Verspätung hatten,
erzählte er Märchen aus Tausend-
undeiner Nacht.

Er verstand es nie,
richtig zu grüßen. Auf guten Tag
sagte er immer: Vielleicht.

Man weiß: er zog seinen Hut
vor den Hunden.
Seine Königskrone aus Zeitungspapier
trugen die Kinder nach Hause.

Der Fünfzeiler im Ortsteil der Zeitung
schloß mit den Worten: Es war
seine letzte Nacht,
als er im Park auf den Baum stieg.

Gerüchte gehen, er habe vergessen
sich festzuhalten,
als er den Friedensappell
an die Welt sprach.

Herbst-Werbung

Hier sehen Sie den Herbst! Ein Freund
jeder Familie, die Hausfrau
schätzt seinen sparsamen
Blätterverbrauch. Ohne Nachnahme
stellt er sich ein, und wenn du
genug von ihm hast,
erstattet er dir selbstverständlich
den vollen Betrag. (Riskiere den Herbst
in bequemen Monatsraten!)

*

Nein nein, der Herbst,
von Meisterhand geschaffen,
hat es nicht nötig, Modell zu stehn
für altdeutsche Möbel
in Nußbaum. Bei ihm ist sowieso
jedes Stück schöner
als das andre. Er bringt siebentausend
Angebote, manche auch
farbig.

Beizeiten
sorgt er für Ordnung,
und träumende Straßenfeger
bekommen von ihm kostenlose Antwort
auf viele Fragen.

Von den Zeugnissen

Der Lehrer sagt: Die Blätter
fallen zur Erde. Wer fällt zur Erde? Wer oder was
bedeckt wen oder was? Ah, das gefällt euch wohl nicht,
wenn ich frage: Wen oder was bedecken die Blätter? Also,
die Erde wird zugedeckt von den Blättern. Die Erde
und außerdem wer oder was? Und wann?
Und wie oft? So, nun schreibt
euren Aufsatz über
den Herbst.

Tageslauf eines dicken Mannes

Morgens
verdingt er sich bei den Kindern am Buddelplatz.
Er beginnt seine Arbeit und sagt: Liebe Kinder,
dieser Bauch ist kein Bauch, sondern der große Berg Bimbula.
Da lachen die Kinder, schlagen Purzelbäume und sagen:
Bitte, großer Berg, morgen mußt du wiederkommen.

Mittags
macht er seine Urwaldfreunde nach.
Er trommelt dann auf seinen Bauch
und manchmal springt er schweren Herzens
auf den Rücken eines Generals und sagt:
Wenn du meinen Bauch mit einer Trommel verwechselst,
so ist das deine eigne klägliche Sache! Dieser Bauch
ist nämlich der große Berg Bimbula,
dessen Schönheit du nie erkennen wirst.

Abends
wird er immer sehr traurig.
Er setzt sich unter die Sterne
und trinkt zehn Liter Himmelsbier.
Manche Leute haben ihn singen gehört —
er singt dann ganz einfältig,
so einfältig, wie's ihm niemand zugetraut hätte:
Mutter, ach Mutter, mich hungert!

Beichte

Seit du fortgegangen bist,
bestelle ich jedesmal zwei Schnäpse statt einen.
Es könnte ja sein, du kämst unverhofft
in die Kneipe, weshalb erst
den Wirt aufmerksam machen; Hallo, mein Freund
ist wiedergekommen, schnell einen Schnaps!

So geschieht es, daß ich immer
vorzeitig besoffen bin. So geschieht es,
daß mir eine neue Ausrede
einfallen muß,
wenn du
zurückkommst.

Bemerkungen eines Schornsteinfegers

Zur Berufswahl

Ich hatte
als Kind mit beiden
Händen an den
Ofen gefaßt. Danke
hatte der Ofen
gesagt, jetzt wird
meinem Schornstein
warm ums Herz.

Zum Allgemeinbefinden

Haben Sie
mit dem Herzen
zu tun?

Ja, mit Sirenen
auf Dächern.

Zum Zeitgeschehen

Konfetti
wäre schwarz wie
Kohlenruß. Schwarzes
Konfetti
streuen, wenn
der Kanzler
unten
vorbeifährt?

Zu Berufserfahrungen

Sie wissen ja, wie klein
die Vögel
aussehen von hier
oben! Mit der Hand
nicht zu greifen. (Mit
dem Federhalter.)

Zu Lohnfragen

Ich liebe
meine Häuser, denn
als Schornsteinfeger
kenne ich
ihr Inneres
besser als jeder
andere.

Zur Altersversorgung

Bewaffnete
Flugzeuge werden
von solchen Personen
gesteuert,
wie sie überall
zu finden sind
als Opfer
fahrlässiger
Berufsberatung.

Brief des Vaters
an den klugen Briefkasten

Eigentlich sollte mein Sohn
   Kälte-Ingenieur werden, aber da kamen dann
die Spaziergänge mit den Papierblumen
   dazwischen. (Er war als zwanzigjähriger
in ein Kinderfest geraten.)

Jeden Abend versuche ich nun, seinen Firlefanz
   madig zu machen. Ich lache ihn aus, biete ihm
Maulschellen an, hol ihn ans Fenster, sage zu ihm: Steh
   nicht so da! Gefällt dir unsere Autobahn
oder gefällt sie dir nicht?

Vergangene Woche sprang er aufs Fensterbrett, flog
   siebzehn Runden hin und her über Wilmersdorf
und verschwand in der Nacht.

Morgens (beim Frühstück) wieder unbegreifliches
   Zeug: er habe Herrn von Lilienthal interviewt,
dem ja die Vögel das Fliegen verdanken
   und die letzten fünfzig Jahre
so manchen Gruß aus der Luft.

(Was meint er damit? Und woher
   die Fähigkeit zu fliegen? Bitte
antworten Sie mir. Ich bin es gewohnt, mich abzufinden
   mit Tatsachen.)

Alte Stätten

1

Wenn Sie
demnächst wieder
in unsere Stadt kommen —
gleich linkerhand: weit und breit
der schönste
Behördenbau!

2

Guten Tag, Windmühlen! Mein Vater
Sancho Pansa
hat mir viel
von euch erzählt.

3

Wir stellen
ungelernte Männer ein! Stellen
sie ein, legen sie ein, salzen sie
ein. So nachzulesen
in einer Soldatenanwerbung
aus rauher Zeit.

Müllerballade

für Hauke Brodersen

1

Mein Vater besaß einen Esel, mich nämlich, der
   war doch recht faul und war allzu faul, um Säcke
und andere Lasten zu tragen. Deshalb sprach mein
   Vater zu mir: Wer unsere Mühle nicht liebt, den
kann ich auch nicht mehr lieben, verschwinde!

2

Zehn volle Jahre und fünfunddreißig siebentägige
   Wochen verbrachte ich nun auf dieser Erde
unter einer dunklen Sonne. Ich gestehe, nicht ein
   einziges Mal hatte ich Lust, das Lied vom
wandernden Müller zu singen, ich sang
   das Lied vom wandernden Esel
sehr oft.

3

Denn besonders auf die Nerven ging mir zunächst
   jene Verszeile: *Die Steine selbst so schwer
sie sind, sie wandern!* Nach und nach aber fand ich
   Gefallen daran, Steine auszustatten mit
Schuhwerk und Wanderbibel. So entstand mein Essay
   über den Spaß von den Anfängen bis zur Gegenwart,
die von solchen Geschichten nichts wissen will.

4

Meine Vorlesung im germanistischen Seminar
    wäre besser beurteilt worden, hätte ich anläßlich
eines kleinen Banketts
    nicht zu sehr
aus der Mühle geplaudert.

5

Heute, in dieser Stunde, bin ich zurückgekommen. Die
    Mühle ist leer, mein Vater nirgends zu sehn. Ich
frage euch alle: Wo seid ihr bloß alle? Die Mühle
    ist arbeitslos, ich warte auf euch. Oder
eßt ihr kein richtiges Brot mehr?

Ein neues Gesetz

*räume den Generalen das Recht ein, lebenslänglich ihre
Toten zu behalten und zu betreuen*

1

Der General nimmt den Abschied, das neue Gesetz
  macht ihm zu schaffen: er wohnt
bei den Toten, jeden begräbt er, jeden
  Hügel formt er mit Schaufel und Spaten, jede
  Blume pflanzt er, in jeden Grabstein schlägt er den
  Namen —
gebückt jeden Tag
  früh, mittags, spät
  arbeitet er zwischen den Gräbern, gebückt
arbeitet er, niemand bringt
  Wasser heran, niemand
  harkt diese Wege, er geht sie allein, schmal, das Unkraut
  führt ihn die Wege entlang, er sagt: Das Unkraut
schießt auf mich zu, es wird von den Toten gesät. Das neue
Gesetz macht ihm zu schaffen.

2

Der General wohnt bei den Toten, er hat Anspruch auf sie.
  Nicht einer, den er nicht kennt, der
  ihn nicht weckt
  jeden Tag
früh, wenn er schläft, Gesicht zur Erde, flach
  zwischen den Gräbern, Befehle
  träumt, Erdreich
  unter der Zunge, nicht einer, der
  ihn nicht hört, keiner verläßt ihn, also
bis in den Tod bleiben sie treu, das macht ihm zu schaffen.

3

Der General hat für seine Toten zu sorgen, er hat sie
    geführt, er hat gehalten,
    was er versprach, es blieb
für jeden erfolgreich. Ein jeder gönnt ihm
    das neue Gesetz: Die Toten
gehören ihm ganz, seht, er schleppt
    Wasser heran, er gießt ihre Hügel, gebückt
arbeitet er zwischen den Gräbern, er hat Anspruch darauf.

4

Der General ist ein Wohltäter hier. Aufrichtig, in besten
    Jahren ein Mann, ruft er
    nach künftigen Gräbern, wo man das Unkraut
    beseitigt. Ein Vorbild, hilft er
den Frauen und Müttern, er sieht,
    ihre Macht
früh, mittags, spät, jeden Tag —
    ihre Macht
    vergaßen sie längst, ihre Söhne, Gesicht
    zur Erde, Erdreich
unter der Zunge, das hält sie nicht wach, der Staub
    an den Fenstern macht ihnen zu schaffen: Ohne Teppich
kein Zuhause, das versteht jede Hausfrau.

5

Der General nimmt den Abschied, das neue Gesetz
    bringt ihn zurück in die Gräben, er hört
    Verdun
    im sanften Touristen-Sommer von Warschau, im
    Wolfsblut der russischen Steppe, er spürt
diesen Tod, der antritt, ihn lebenslänglich
    zu töten, also verwirft er
das neue Gesetz, in keinen Grabstein schlägt er den Namen.

6

Der General, in dieser Stunde ein Mann, verbindlich, treu
    seiner Arbeit, Söhne
    zu liefern ans Erdreich
früh, mittags, spät, jede Nacht —
    jetzt
in diesem Jahrhundert
    klinkt er sein Lächeln aus: *Für den Einsatz
    auf kleinere Städte
    bewährt sich der mittlere Bombentyp.* Das sagt er, clever,
ein guter Geschäftsmann. Und diese Bezeichnung gilt noch
                                    ein Weilchen.

Rat des Sozialamtes

Wenn Sie
keine Arbeit finden,
dann sollten Sie
schlafen
und überwintern. Sie
haben dadurch
die seltene Möglichkeit,
einigen Tieren
näherzukommen.

Ein alter König
schaut ins Familienalbum

Dieses Foto
  zeigt meine Eule und mich. Es stammt
aus der Vergangenheit. Trotzdem erkenne ich uns wieder
  und natürlich sehe ich auch, wie uns
damals zumute war.

Es zeigt
  einen König, die Krone
sitzt auf dem Kopf, meine Augen sind lustig, ich sehe mich
  lächeln. Der Mund ist der Mund eines Menschen, der Spaß
daran hat, König zu sein. Mein Mantel
  ist rot, die Jacke, das Wams, beide sind blau, die
Hände übereinandergelegt, sie hatten
  wenig zu tun, das bißchen Zeptergehalte, hier
und da mal ein Wink, ich hatte Bedeutendes
  nicht zu regieren. Als das Foto geknipst wurde, stand
mein Volk unterm Balkon, aber lassen wir das.

Gleich neben mir, rechts:
  meine Eule. Auch sie
hat Glück in den Augen. Sie lebt
  nicht mehr. Die Krone hängt am Garderobenständer,
das hätte ihr Freude gemacht.

Alles in allem: Ein komisches Bild. (Wir sollten uns
  kein Bein ausreißen darüber, daß wir
abgesetzt wurden.)

Erlernter Beruf eines Vogels

1

Gut geschlafen hat der Vogel im Vogelhaus. Er öffnet
die Augen, er freut sich auf etwas sehr Schönes, er sagt:
Sehr schön sind Wasser und Körner, er frühstückt Wasser
und Körner. Das macht ihn fröhlich, er tanzt, er holt
seinen Hut, hebt die Flügel und fliegt.

2

Im Fliegen sagt er: Ich flieg über ein sehr schönes Land,
da unten frühstückt ein Mensch, ich werde ihm sagen:
Sehr schön ist ein Mensch, der ohne Pickelhaube frühstücken
kann, nicht minder ein Land, das den Menschen in jede
Vogelrichtung sprechen, schauen, frühstücken läßt.

3

So, sagt der Vogel, das war recht einfach gesagt, aber es
mußte gesagt sein, denn solche Klarstellung gehört ins
Kapitel der Freiheit, will sagen, zum erlernten Beruf
eines Vogels.

Jetzt im Frühjahr

Der Trapezkünstler Heinrich B., reisender
    Akrobat und Schausteller, zog im letzten September
mit seiner Frau, seinem Bruder und zwei
    schulpflichtigen Kindern in die
Vorstadt von S. Fünfzig Plakate, keins größer
    als eine Zeitung, kündigten an: Heinrich B. —
den Menschen des Himmels.

Die erste Vorstellung
war angezeigt auf einen Sonntag. Der Ort: ein
Ruinengrundstück. Die Arbeit am Seil, im Höhepunkt
    der Handstand auf gestapelten
Stühlen, wurde begutachtet von vier
    Personen: von der Frau, vom
Bruder und zwei schulpflichtigen Kindern
    des Trapezkünstlers Heinrich B. Andere Besucher
waren nicht gekommen.

Jetzt im Frühjahr
    entdecke ich eins der Plakate
am Eingang zur Kohlenhalde. Nicht größer
    als eine Zeitung, hat es den Winter überstanden
mit der Vorschau auf den Menschen des Himmels.

Legitimation

Ich wohne hinter den Schritten
des Polizisten, der meinen Paß kontrolliert.
Ich wohne im Keller einer mittelgroßen
Ruine, im Altersheim
für den pensionierten Wind.

Ich wohne im pendelnden Käfig
eines Papageis, der alle Gesetzbücher
auswendig lernt.

Meine Behausung
am Platz für öffentliche Unordnung
ist der brennende Zirkus —
meine Grüße
gehen auf Händen zu dir hinüber,
meine Grüße
sind die letzten Akrobaten
unter der brennenden Kuppel.

aus **Brevier eines Degenschluckers**

Mein Herr, sagte eine Laterne zu mir, Sie dürfen mir glauben, ich wollte eine gute Laterne sein! Man hat vergessen, daß ich ein Galgen war. Das Blut ist nicht abgewaschen, der trockne Strick vergiftet den Wind. Bedenken Sie bitte: Jede Nacht das wiederkehrende Bild, ein Soldat unter dem Gaslicht, die Füße gestreckt, das Schild auf der Brust.

Ich konnte den Selbstmord dieser Laterne nicht mehr verhindern. Sie zerrte sich selbst ihr einziges Bein aus der Erde, sie hüpfte in lächerlich kurzen Sprüngen zur Brücke: der Schlag ans Geländer! Der Aufschrei der Fische! Sie fiel kopfüber in den Kanal.

*

Ordnung muß sein, sprach der Anarchist und warf die Bombe ins Rathaus.

*

Bei Schneefall tanzen die Hunde zweibeinig ohne Dressur. Sie sprechen: Schnee, Schnee, bleib noch lange hier! dort oben ist die Hundehütte ohne Maulkorb, von dort kommen Sterne und schmecken nach Brot.

Ihre lachenden Mäuler scharren einen Weg durch den Schneeberg Erde, ihre Sprünge sind stummes Gebell, ihr Leben ist mit dem Schnee auf die Erde gekommen.

*

Als die Erde sich im Schlaf von der einen auf die andre Seite
warf, sah ich die Kriege tief geduckt springen von Land zu
Land, Bomben und Zündschnüre im Mantel wie die Räuber
einer Operettenbühne, angetan mit puderweißen Masken.

Wie schrecklich die Täuschung war, wie falsch das Bild, sah ich
erst, als die Erde, zu Tode getroffen im Schlaf, sich zurück auf
die andere Seite warf.

Cagliostros letzter Zauberspruch
an seine Freunde

Ist es schon soweit, habt ihr auch alles zusammengetragen, jeden Koffer gepackt und nichts vergessen? — auch nicht den kostbaren Drachenhut, der den schönen erfrischenden Regen schickt?

Ich sehe, ihr habt alles vorbereitet, ich werde jetzt gehn. Behaltet die Formel, die aus den Särgen alter und neuer Langeweile Kleinholz macht. Bettet den Freund und den Feind, die nicht mehr nach Hause kommen, wenn der Totengräber, der Staub, zu wandern beginnt.

Lebt wohl! Auf den Namen der Wolken getauft, fliege ich ohne Passierschein über das Aufgebot der Schatten. Ich trage den Drachenhut, der den schönen erfrischenden Regen schickt, denn ich muß durch das Feuer, das mich draußen erwartet.

Tod des Tänzers

Er kommt durch die Straßen, alle Leute erkennen ihn, er schwingt eine Zeitung, er hat sie gelesen, er hüpft über Autos, klettert an Dachrinnen entlang und ruft: O Leute, nun freut euch mit mir, der Staatshenker ist wieder im Amt! Nun gelangt endlich Sinn in unser Leben, wir wollen vergnügt sein. Nun weiß ein jeder, wofür er sich plagt. Der Lohn ist ihm sicher. Auf, auf, sprecht mir nach: Unser Kopf gehört dem Henker, dem Mann der altbewährten Ordnung!

Sie sammeln sich alle zum Chor, sie sprechen: Wem sonst . . . als nur dem Mann der altbewährten Ordnung!

Der Tänzer faltet verwundert die Zeitung zusammen. Sie lächeln, sie küssen und liebkosen sich, sie sind ein Reigen der Zufriedenheit. Der Tänzer tanzt nicht mit.

Er läuft ihnen nach und schreit: Hört mich an, ihr habt die Sache wörtlich genommen! Die Freiheit wird verkümmern, die Wahrheit verbluten!

Da rücken sie gegen ihn vor und machen Fäuste aus ihren Händen. Sie rufen, während sie schlagen: Du beleidigst den Henker, den Mann der Barmherzigkeit, der uns von der Freiheit erlöst!

Sie lächeln wieder, küssen und liebkosen sich, und der Tänzer stirbt inmitten ihrer Dankprozession.

Steckbriefe

1

Gesucht wird ein Regen,
der das Gift aus den Augen spült.

Gesucht wird ein stelzenlaufendes Kind,
das dem Regen hohe Belohnung verspricht.

2

Der Fensterputzer
lehnt seine Leiter an den verstaubten Himmel.
Der Herbst öffnet die Synagoge —
die Stürme singen den Thoratext.

Rauchzeichen bei Tag.

Die Bäume sind alte Rabbiner,
sie zünden die Leuchter an.

Feuerzeichen bei Nacht

Die Ketten
sind um den Schlafbaum der Krähen gelegt.
Das Gebell der Hunde sagt deine Träume voraus.
Die Windmühle des Kindes
spricht das Urteil über die Welt.